UTILIZING YOUR 8760 HOURS OF A YEAR EFFECTIVELY

YOU CAN SUCCEED IN LIFE REGARDLESS OF YOUR BACKGROUND, TRIBE, RACE, BELIEVE OR EDUCATION

Copyright © 2018. All Rights Reserved.

No part of this publication may be reproduced, distributed, or transmitted in any form or by any means, including photocopying, recording, or other electronic or mechanical methods, or by any information storage and retrieval system without the prior written permission of the publisher, except in the case of very brief quotations embodied in critical reviews and certain other noncommercial uses permitted by copyright law.

Why You Should Read This Book

Although the rich do get richer, these book is to remind us that through determination and grit anyone can overcome their circumstances and achieve extraordinary success regardless of their status in life.

This book will show you that the real way to success is how you spend your 8760 hours in a year, not you background,race,education or believe, by providing you the right guardian to overcome. Consequently improviing your overall life...

TABLE OF CONTENTS

Chapter 1. INTRODUCTION

Chapter 2. Harlan Sanders

Chapter 3. Warren Buffett

Chapter 4. Richard Branson

Chapter 5. Kenny Troutt

Chapter 6. Starbucks' Howard Schultz

Chapter 7. Ken Langone

Chapter 8. Oprah Winfrey

Chapter 9. Shahid Khan

Chapter 10. Kirk Kerkorian

chapter 11 John Paul DeJoria

chapter 12 Do Won Chang

chapter 13. Ralph Lauren

chapter 14. mogul Francois Pinault

chap ter 15. Leonardo Del Vecchio

chapter 16. Li Ka-shing

chapter 17. Harold Simmons

chapter 18. Oracle's Larry Ellison

chapter 19. Andrew Carnegie

chapter 20. Qoutes from successful peoples

chapter 21. Here are 7 undeniable reasons why some people fail where others succeed

chapter 21, conclusion

Wealth tends to create more wealth, but a rich background is not the only way to the top. Some of the world's wealthiest people started out dirt poor.

All from humble beginnings, these people not only climbed to the top of their industries but also became some of the richest people in the world.

Just like food is incomplete and tasteless without spice, my efforts to explain and outline success here would be tasteless or meaningless without the success stories in my mind that have inspired me. Below are a list of the most successful people who started from nothing and earn millions and billions today.

Harlan Sanders

KFC founder Colonel Sanders didn't achieve his remarkable rise to success until his 60s

The real Col. Sanders was an entrepreneur who didn't become a professional chef until he was 40, didn't franchise Kentucky Fried Chicken until he was 62, and didn't become an icon until after he sold his company at 75.

According to a 1970 New Yorker profile by William Whitworth, as well as biographies from Bio and the University of Houston, here are the highlights of the Colonel's remarkable rise to success.

Harland Sanders was born in 1890 and grew up on a farm in Indiana. When he was 6 years old, Sanders' father died, leaving him to take care of his younger brother and sister while his mom spent long days working. One of these responsibilities was feeding his siblings, and by age 7 he was already a decent cook, according to the New Yorker.

His mom remarried when he was 12. Because his new stepfather didn't like the boys around, Sanders' brother was sent to live with an aunt while he was sent to work on a farm about 80 miles away.

Sanders soon realized he would rather work all day than go to school, so he dropped out in the seventh grade.

In addition to a stint in Cuba with the Army, Sanders spent the first half of his life working a series of odd jobs, including stoking the steam engines of trains throughout the South, selling insurance, selling tires, making lighting systems, and operating a ferry boat.

He acquired a service station in Corbin, Kentucky, in 1930 and began serving classic Southern dishes to travelers. The location became known for its food, and Sanders eventually got rid of the service station's gas pump and converted the location to a full-fledged restaurant.

His breakthrough came in 1939 when he found that frying his chicken and its signature "11 herbs and spices" in a new device, a pressure cooker (different from the ones used today), resulted in the ideal consistency he had been looking for.

Sanders' restaurant enjoyed great popularity over the next decade, and in 1950 the governor of Kentucky named him colonel, the highest title of honor the state can give. Sanders began dressing the part, adopting the white suit and Kentucky colonel tie that would help make him a pop-culture icon.

In 1952, he made a deal with his restaurateur friend, Pete Harman, to sell his chicken dish as "Kentucky Fried Chicken" in exchange for a 4-cent royalty on every piece sold. After it became a top-selling item, Sanders made the same deal with several other local restaurants.

Things were going great, but when a new interstate bypassed Sanders' restaurant, it spelled doom.

He sold the location at a loss in 1956, leaving his $105 monthly Social Security check as his only income. Sanders then decided that he was not going to settle for a quiet retirement.

kfc sign

A KFC and Sanders Cafe sign at the site of Sanders' Corbin, Kentucky, restaurant where he developed his signature fried chicken.

Since he'd closed his restaurant, the Colonel decided to dedicate himself fully to the franchising side project he'd started four years earlier.

He hit the road with his wife, the car packed with a couple pressure cookers, flour, and spice blends. He would enter a restaurant, offer to cook his chicken, and then make a deal if the owner liked what they tasted.

By 1963, Sanders was fielding franchise requests without having to put in the legwork, and had more than 600 restaurants across the US and Canada selling Kentucky Fried Chicken. That October, he was approached by John Y. Brown, Jr., "an aggressive young lawyer" as the New Yorker puts it, and a venture capitalist named Jack C. Massey who wanted to buy the franchise rights.

Sanders was initially reluctant, but after weeks of persuasion, he agreed to sell his rights for $2 million ($15.1 million in 2015 dollars) in January 1965, and the deal went through in March.

Under the contract, the company Kentucky Fried Chicken would establish its own restaurants around the world and would not compromise the chicken recipe. Sanders was to have a lifetime salary of $40,000 (later upped to $75,000), a seat on the board, majority ownership of KFC's Canadian franchises, and would serve as the company's brand ambassador.

Sanders wasn't happy to let go of his baby, but at 75, he decided that it would be best to see his company continue to grow beyond his capacity.

The New Yorker profile noted that some of his friends believed Sanders was shorted on the deal, but it also shows that Sanders turned down stock in the company and did not negotiate for a higher price.

It seems Sanders' pursuit was never really about becoming rich, but rather about becoming renowned for his food. That's why he constantly grumbled and swore about the more profitable but lower quality gravy that the corporate KFC began producing.

"If you were a franchisee turning out perfect gravy but making very little money for the company and I was a franchisee making lots of money for the company but serving gravy that was merely excellent, the Colonel would think that you were great and I was a bum," a KFC executive told the New Yorker. "With the Colonel, it isn't money that counts, it's artistic talent."

Sanders spent the latter years of his life giving interviews on talk shows and appearing in commercials, like this one from 1969:

The University of Houston, which honors Sanders in its Hospitality Industry Hall of Fame, says that up until his death in 1980, the Colonel traveled 250,000 miles each year visiting KFC locations and promoting the brand in the media.

Brown, who sold his stake in KFC in 1971 for $284 million, became governor of Kentucky in 1979. When Sanders died the next year, Brown said Sanders was "a real legend" and "the spirit of the American dream," the New York Times reported.

Sanders may have lacked the motivation to become as wealthy as he could have been, but he's now known in 115 countries for his favorite fried chicken recipe, which is more than he ever could have hoped for when he hit the road at age 65 with a car full of cooking supplies.

Warren Buffett

Warren Edward Buffett was born on August 30, 1930 in Omaha, Nebraska, to Howard, a stockbroker and future congressman, and Leila (Stahl) Buffett. As a child, Buffett reportedly showed interest in stocks, writing stock prices on the chalk board in his father's office. Legend has it that he told his childhood friend if he wasn't a millionaire by age 30, he would jump off of the tallest building in Omaha. When Buffett was 11 years old, he visited the New York Stock Exchange and bought his first shares: three shares of Cities Service Preferred (an oil and gas concern) for himself and three for his sister Doris.

Nebraska was hit hard by the effects of the Great Depression. Like many children of the Depression, Buffett grew up to respect the value of money. He became so frugal that when he moved to New York for business school, he lived at the YMCA in order to save money. He got a job as a paperboy when he was 13 years old, and would eventually deliver newspapers on both the morning and afternoon routes. In 1944, Warren filed his first tax return and reached his short-term goal of having $1,000.

Buffett spent his formative adolescence in Washington, D.C., where he graduated from Woodrow Wilson High School. In grade school and high school Buffett not only showed his precocious proclivity for business by delivering newspapers, but also sold stamps, Coca-Cola (KO) beverages, golf balls and magazines door-to-door, while also working as an editor for a horse racing tip sheet called Stable-Boy Selections. During this period, Warren started a pinball leasing business. He and a business partner bought cheap pinball machines, ensured they were in working order, and then installed them to get what were, quite possibly, his high school classmates' coins.

By the time he was 15, Warren had amassed $2,000 and used it to buy a 40-acre farm in Nebraska. He hired a farm laborer to work on the land, then used the profits to help pay his way through University. Warren graduated with a Bachelor of Science degree from the University of Nebraska, Lincoln, after which he applied to Harvard Business School. After being rejected by Harvard, Warren matriculated at Columbia Business School, where he graduated in 1951 with a Master of Science in Economics. While at Columbia, Warren studied under legendary value investor Benjamin Graham.

With his degree in hand, Warren returned to Omaha and studied public speaking while there. He also began teaching investing at the University of Nebraska, Omaha. In 1954, Warren moved his new wife Susan and his young daughter to New York, where he began working for his mentor, Benjamin Graham.

After several years of moving from city to city, Warren permanently returned to Omaha and bought himself a modest house. For someone as frugal as Warren, the $31,500 price tag on the house was difficult for him to accept and he nicknamed the decision Buffett's Folly.

From 1951 to 1956, Warren was an investment salesman and a securities analyst. By 1956, he had $174,000 and a house, and decided to retire at 26 years of age, under the belief that he could make enough money from his investments alone to live a comfortable life. Warren realized, however, that to meet his goal of becoming a millionaire by age 35, he would have to be more active.

warren Buffett's name is practically synonymous with his biggest success: Berkshire Hathaway (BRK.A). Warren became an integral part of Berkshire Hathaway in the early 1960s and helped the company expand into one of the largest conglomerates in the world. In 1956, his path to success began to accelerate when he moved back to Nebraska with his family.

Before working for Benjamin Graham, Warren had been an investment salesman – a job that he liked doing, except when the stocks he suggested dropped in value and lost money for his clients. To minimize the potential of having irate clients, Warren started a partnership with his close friends and family. The partnership had unique restrictions attached to it: Warren himself would invest only $100 and, through re-invested management fees, would grow his stake in the partnership. Warren would take half of the partnerships gains over 4% and would repay the partnership a quarter of any loss incurred. Furthermore, money could only be added or withdrawn from the partnership on December 31st, and partners would have no input about the investments in the partnership.

By 1959, Warren had opened a total of seven partnerships and had a 9.5% stake in more than a million dollars of partnership assets. Three years later, Warren was now a millionaire and merged all of his partnerships into a single entity.

In 1962, Warren saw an opportunity to invest in a New England textile company called Berkshire Hathaway and bought some of its stock. Warren began to aggressively buy shares after a dispute with its management convinced him that the company needed a change in leadership. Ironically, the purchase of Berkshire Hathaway is one of Warren's major regrets. (For more, see: Always Bet On Berkshire Hathaway.)

Understanding the beauty of owning insurance companies – clients pay premiums today to possibly receive payments decades later – Warren used Berkshire Hathaway as a holding company to buy National Indemnity Company (the first of many insurance companies he would buy) and used its substantial cash flow to finance further acquisitions.

As a value investor, Warren is a sort of Jack-of-all-trades when it comes to industry knowledge. Berkshire Hathaway is a great example. Buffett saw a company that was cheap and bought it, regardless of the fact that he wasn't an expert in textile manufacturing. Over the decades, Warren has bought, held and sold companies in a variety of different industries.

Some of Berkshire Hathaway's most well-known subsidiaries are, but not limited to, GEICO (yes, that little Gecko belongs to Warren Buffett), Dairy Queen, NetJets, Benjamin Moore & Co., and Fruit of the Loom. Again, these are only a handful of companies of which Berkshire Hathaway has a majority share.

The company also has interests in many other companies, including American Express Co. (AXP), Costco Wholesale Corp. (COST), DirectTV (DTV), General Electric Co. (GE), General Motors Co. (GM), Coca-Cola Co. (KO), International Business Machines Corp. (IBM), Wal-Mart Stores Inc. (WMT), Proctor & Gamble Co. (PG) and Wells Fargo & Co. (WFC).

In more recent years, Buffett has acted as a financier and facilitator of major transactions. During the Great Recession, Warren invested and lent money to companies that were facing financial disaster. Seven years later, the effects of these transactions are surfacing and they're enormous:

A loan to Mars Inc. resulted in a $680 million profit

Wells Fargo & Co. (WFC), of which Berkshire Hathaway bought almost 120 million shares during the Great Recession, is up 6.75 times from its 2009 low

American Express Co. (AXP) is up about five times since Warren's investment in 2008

Bank of America Corp. (BAC) pays $300 million a year and Berkshire Hathaway has the option to buy additional shares at around $7 each – less than half of what it trades at today

Goldman Sachs Group Inc. (GS) paid out $500 million in dividends a year and a $500 million redemption bonus when they repurchased the shares.

Most recently, Warren has partnered up with 3G Capital to merge J.H. Heinz Company and Kraft Foods to create the Kraft Heinz Food Company (KHC). The new company is the third largest food and beverage company in North America and fifth largest in the world, and boasts annual revenues of $28 billion.

Modesty and quiet living meant that it took Forbes some time to notice Warren and add him to the list of richest Americans, but when they finally did in 1985, he was already a billionaire. Early investors in Berkshire Hathaway could have bought in as low as $275 a share and by 2014 the stock price had reached $200,000.

It not about where you come from, nor your background , it's about determination and focus.

Richard Branson

Entrepreneur Richard Branson launched Virgin Records in 1973. Today Virgin Group holds more than 200 companies in more than 30 countries.

Richard Branson was born on July 18, 1950, in Surrey, England, Richard Branson struggled in school and dropped out at age 16—a decision that ultimately lead to the creation of Virgin Records. His entrepreneurial projects started in the music industry and expanded into other sectors making Branson a billionaire. His Virgin Group holds more than 200 companies, including the recent Virgin Galactic, a space-tourism company. Branson is also known for his adventurous spirit and sporting achievements, including crossing oceans in a hot air balloon.

Richard Charles Nicholas Branson was born on July 18, 1950, in Surrey, England. His father, Edward James Branson, worked as a barrister. His mother, Eve Branson, was employed as a flight attendant. Richard, who struggled with dyslexia, had a hard time with educational institutions. He nearly failed out of the all-boys Scaitcliffe School, which he attended until the age of 13. He then transferred to Stowe School, a boarding school in Stowe, Buckinghamshire, England.

Still struggling, Branson dropped out at the age of 16 to start a youth-culture magazine called Student. The publication, run by students, for students, sold $8,000 worth of advertising in its first edition, which was launched in 1966. The first run of 50,000 copies was disseminated for free, after Branson covered the costs with advertising.

By 1969, Branson was living in a London commune, surrounded by the British music and drug scene. It was during this time that Branson had the idea to begin a mail-order record company called Virgin to help fund his magazine efforts. The company performed modestly, but made Branson enough that he was able to expand his business venture, adding a record shop in Oxford Street, London. With the success of the record shop, the high school drop-out was able to build a recording studio in 1972 in Oxfordshire, England.

His first artist on the Virgin Records label, Mike Oldfield, recorded his single "Tubular Bells" in 1973 with the help of Branson's team. The song was an instant smash, staying on the UK charts for 247 weeks. Using the momentum of Oldfield's success, Branson then signed other aspiring musical groups to label, including the Sex Pistols. Artists such as the Culture Club, the Rolling Stones, and Genesis would follow, helping to make Virgin Music one of the top six record companies in the world.

Branson expanded his entrepreneurial efforts yet again, this time to include the travel company the Voyager Group in 1980, the airline Virgin Atlantic in 1984, and a series of Virgin Megastores. But Branson's success was not always predictable. By 1992, Virgin was suddenly struggling to stay financially afloat. The company was sold later that year to THORN EMI for $1 billion.

Branson was crushed by the loss, reportedly crying after the contract was signed, but remained determined to stay in the music business. In 1993, he founded the station Virgin Radio, and several years later he started a second record company, V2. Founded in 1996, V2 now includes artists such as Powder Finger and Tom Jones.

Branson's Virgin Group now holds more than 200 companies in more than 30 countries, including the United Kingdom, the United States, Australia, Canada, Asia, Europe and South Africa. He has expanded his businesses to include a train company, a luxury game preserve, a mobile phone company and a space-tourism company, Virgin Galactic.

Branson is also known for his sporting achievements, notably the record-breaking Atlantic crossing in Virgin Atlantic Challenger II in 1986, and the first crossing by hot-air balloon of the Atlantic (1987) and Pacific (1991). He was knighted in 1999 for his contribution to entrepreneurship, and in 2009, he landed at No. 261 on Forbes' "World Billionaires" list with his $2.5 billion in self-made fortune, which includes two private islands.

In recent years, the ever-adventurous Branson has focused much of his attention on his space tourism venture. He partnered with Scaled Composites to form The Spaceship Company, which is currently developing a suborbital spaceplane, and, in April 2013, the project made an impressive leap forward with the test launch of SpaceShipTwo.

Branson was delighted by the success of his spaceship's first test, telling NBC News that "We're absolutely delighted that it broke the sound barrier on its very first flight, and that everything went so smoothly." He expects to be finishing testing the craft by the end of 2013. By April 2013, more than 500 people had bought their tickets for Virgin Galactic's voyages.

Indid there is no smooth way to success but with ditermination, focus and hard work you can also be successful.

Kenny Troutt

Net worth: $1.7 billion (as of Sept. 2013)

Kenny A. Troutt was born in 1948 and is the founder of the very celebrated excels communications which can be defined as the teas based Telecommunication Company that utilizes multi-level marketing services to offer out their major products to the targeted audience.

He became one of the richest people on earth during the year 1998 when he sold Teleglobe in which his share was unsettled. But he had to come a very long way to become such a rich person. He is a son of a local bartender. His studies were done in the Illinois University, for which he used to arrange the money by selling insurance to different people. It is because of his hard-work and exertions, he's now involve in horse racing, stock selling and bonds retailing etc.

Though his classmates from school and college wanted to become doctors, teachers or firefighters but Kenny A. Troutt always knew what he wanted to be. Being the oldest among all of his siblings and struggling in the Illinois family, he once told his teacher he wanted to be really rich. And after he surpassed his own childhood dreams, he became the CEO of the Dallas-based Excel Communications Inc. in which his takes in the entire company were around 50% making his net worth more than 1.5 billion dollars.

He came from a very poor family where there were hardly any accommodations in the house; he now owns a 13,000 square foot country French mansion in his name which is just across the street from the manor of Ross Perot. He has had a true experience of hard knocks and the jolts given by the roller coasters of life, he is entirely aware of the ups and downs, high and low roads of life and even though he is always hoping for the best to happen, he still prepares for the worst case scenarios.

He remembers being broke like its yesterday and with his familiarity of living in house projects he still thinks that he is strange to all the wealth that he has earned. He still hears echoes of his father's voice and it because of the fact that he is now one of the most up-and-coming businessmen of the world. He believes in making schemes since this way he has made the most of his negligible resources in getting what he has today, being a part of luminary life.

His life can surely be taken as an example for all those who are in search of the turning point in their lives, to show that poor background is not a factor when it comes to been successful.

Starbucks' Howard Schultz

Net worth: $2 billion (as of Sept. 2013)

In 1981 Howard Schultz visited the Starbucks coffee shop in Seattle, a client company of his employer at the time, and ever since then their paths have been inseparable. A year later a new employment and a working travel in Italy became the reason for him to give birth to ideas, which would change American society and the way it spends its free time.

Schultz was born 1953 in Brooklyn, New York. He is the son of a truck driver of German and Jewish origin and, together with his two brothers, lived a childhood deprived of luxury. The poor way his father was treated by his employers, the lack of social insurance and benefits, made a great impression to young Schultz. Later, as he successfully graduated from an elite university, the education where he had earned due to his sports achievements, he was bound to make things right for his future employees.

At the time Starbucks was a small Seattle coffee-bean shop. Schultz worked for Xerox, but then switched to the position of general manager for a Swedish drip coffee maker manufacturer, where he had to often make business trips to check how potential and current clients were doing business. The passion of the owners and the amazing smell of fresh coffee he encountered the first time he entered the shop made Schultz wish to start working for Starbucks. His wish was fulfilled and he got the job of a marketing director.

"If you want to build a great enterprise, you have to have the courage to dream great dreams. If you dream small dreams, you may succeed in building something small. For many people, that is enough. But if you want to achieve widespread impact and lasting value, be bold." That's one of is favorite quotes.

A 1982 trip to Italy, however, made him feel discontent with how the institution was doing business. Italian coffee culture inspired Schultz in such a way, that he insisted that Starbucks adopts the Italian cafeteria model: small coffee houses at every corner of every street, which serve cups of coffee, and where clients don't come and go, but spend their free time and accept as social encounter spots. The shop owners failed to see the bright future behind their employee's ideas, an event, which led to him quitting his job and founding his own cafeteria, Il Giornale.

After 3 years of hard work Schultz convinced the Starbucks founders to sell him their retail unit for the sum of $3.8 Million. He immediately renamed the joint coffee brand after the Seattle shop, and aimed towards building one of the most recognizable companies in America. In the 90s the company grew with rapid speed, became public, and multiplied its owner's fortune.

Aside from making a "fast food nation" such as the United States wish to spend hours at a time conversing with friends at a coffee place, Schultz' greatest achievement was actually holding on to the idea of social benefits for employees, which had been denied to his father many years ago. To this day people working at Starbucks are recognized for their loyalty to management.

Starbucks serves coffee, including several cup sizes and instant coffee, tea, fruit juice, baked goods, and salads. It is widening its gamma of products constantly, always trying to reach new horizons. Today most of the Starbucks locations are company-owned. With more than 17,000 stores worldwide many believe that it is a franchise, however, only as an exception Starbucks may enter into contracts with other companies.

Schultz is currently number 311 of the Forbes 400 and has a net worth of $1.5 Billion. He is internationally recognized as a trailblazer both in coffee retail and business management and is famous for his ever existent desire to expand his business and his capabilities, reach new markets, and for his willingness to provide security and comfort for his employees.

Ken Langone

Net worth: $2.1 billion (as of Sept. 2013)

Getting kicked down stairs at a small home-improvement company made Kenneth Langone rich and has saved millions of do-it-yourselfers big bucks.

In 1978, the legendary investor got into a tiff with the top dog at Handy Dan, a small Southern California-based home-improvement company in which he held a small stake. The dispute was resolved by members of Handy Dan's parent company, who bought Langone out, then fired its Chief Executive Officer, Bernard Marcus, and Chief Financial Officer, Arthur Blank.

The trio went to work immediately, launching Home Depot (HD) later that same year. It has since become the world's largest home-improvement chain, with about 2,200 stores in North America, Puerto Rico, and China. It's also the second largest retailer after Walmart (WMT).

Langone's stunning success stories (and Home Depot is just one of them) must have come as a shock to at least one person in his hometown of Roslyn Heights, New York: his high-school principal. The school head had advised Langone's parents not to burn money by sending the unpromising student to college. His father, a plumber, and his mother, a cafeteria worker, disagreed. Instead they mortgaged their house to send their son to Bucknell University in Pennsylvania.

As a college student, Langone worked as a caddy, butcher, and ditch digger to stay afloat. His parents' faith in him and his hard work paid off: He earned a bachelor's degree in economics in about 3.5 years.

After graduation, Langone took a full-time job in the investment department at Equitable Life Assurance company and went to New York University's School of Business four nights a week, earning an MBA in 1960. He also served two years in the US Army.

With his newly minted MBA in hand, Langone next took a job with a small Wall Street company, R.W. Pressprich. As executive vice president, he teamed up with Ross Perot, then an ambitious but unknown Texan on the make and years away from his presidential run as an independent. Langone took Perot's start-up, Electronic Data Systems, public in 1968 at $16.50 a share, or about 118 times earnings. In 2008, Hewlett-Packard (HPQ) acquired Electronic Data Systems for about

$13.9 billion to better compete with International Business Machines (IBM) in the lucrative computer-services field.

In 1974, Langone launched Invemed Associates, a small investment bank, focusing on start-ups in the medical field. The Wall Street firm soon raised $5 million for a medical-electronics company, Ivac. Langone later took over the company and sold it to Eli Lilly (LLY) in a stock transaction in 1977. Ivac became the drug company's multi-billion-dollar medical-instruments division.

The same year that he launched Invemed, Langone bought a seat on the New York Stock Exchange (NYX) for $60,000. He later sold the seat for $1.5 million. In 2005, he led a bid to buy the entire exchange. The move was unsuccessful, but Langone had the right idea: He wanted to rely more heavily on electronic trading to speed execution of buy and sell orders, a tack now followed by the world's largest exchange.

These days, Langone, cognizant of his roots, supports many charitable organizations, including the New York Philharmonic, Ronald McDonald House, and the Damon Runyon Cancer Research Foundation. He's also donated to Bucknell University and New York University and supports Ken's Kids, a Home Depot-affiliated not-for-profit organization that provides jobs for young adults with disabilities.

For aspiring entrepreneurs, Langone's message is simple: work, work, work. After he donated $10 million to New York University, the college named its night business school the Langone Program. The investor has also donated $200 million to the school for its medical center, since renamed The NYU Langone Medical Center.

Seen as a model Italian-American citizen, and "a virtuous man of good character," by the head of Columbus Citizens Foundation, an Italian community group, Langone was named the grand marshal in this year's Italian Day parade in New York City.

"Mr. Langone is living proof that the American dream continues," said Louis Tallarini, president of the Foundation.

And whatever happened to Handy Dan? The short answer: Langone, the unpromising student from Long Island, killed it with a better idea.

Oprah Winfrey

Net worth: $2.9 billion (as of Sept. 2013)

Oprah Winfrey, the richest African American of the 20th century, was born in Kosciusko, Mississippi in 1958, on 29th of January. She is best known as the most successful American television producer, host and philanthropist and is among the most influential women in the world. She did not have a promising childhood and had to face a variety of hardships in her teenage life. After her parents' separation, she was sent to her grandparents, to live in extreme poverty. Some say that she used to wear dresses made of potato sack. She reunited with her mother at the age of 6 who moved with her to Milwaukee, Wisconsin. Her mother spent her all day out working as a maid at households and had no time for little Winfrey. At the age of nine, as she says, she was raped by her cousin, her uncle and a family friend. Having had enough, she ran away from her home at the age of 13 and became mother at 14. After her son's death in infancy, she went back to live with her barber father in

Tennessee. This was the first time, as she remembers she took her studies seriously and managed to become an honors student. Her dedication soon paid off and she became the most popular student at East Nashville High School and won several awards in open speech competition. Later, she studied communication from Tennessee State University.

At the age of 19, her life took a turn for better when she got a job at a local Radio Station as a co-anchor for the local evening news. In 1984, she started to host 'AM Chicago', an early morning talk show, which soon became the most watched show in America. Later, it was renamed as 'The Oprah Winfrey Show'. The syndicated talk show became the most popular show in the Television history with over 30 million American viewers and spanned across 144 countries worldwide. She has also proved herself as the most influential spiritual leader through 'Change Your Life TV' with 22 million female viewers.

Besides being a TV host and producer, she is the co-founder of Oxygen Media and founder of Oprah Magazine. In 1998, she started a charity named "Oprah's Angel Network" for which she carries all administrative costs. Oprah's Angel Network donated $10 million after Hurricane Katrina and collected $11 million given by her viewers on her re□uest. She is regarded as the 32nd most philanthropist person in the world. In 2005, Business Week enlisted her name among 50 most generous philanthropists for her contribution which was equivalent to $303 million dollars. According to Forbes of 2009, her net worth is $2.7 billion dollar.

At the 2002 Emmy Award, she was the recipient of first Bob Hope Humanitarian Award for her contribution to Television and Films.

QUOTES

"My philosophy is that not only are you responsible for your life, but doing the best at this moment puts you in the best place for the next moment." – Oprah Winfrey

Shahid Khan

Net worth: $3.8 billion (as of Sept. 2013)

A well-known businessman born on July 18, 1950, Shahid Khan (alias Shad Khan) was born in Lahore in Pakistan. His passion to make money and become successful brought him to America. English Football League Championship team Fulham F.C., Jacksonville Jaguars of the National Football League and Flex-N-Gate are a few big names the billionaire is associated with.

At the age of 16, Khan first moved to the US with a dream of turning an architect. He dropped the idea soon after finishing first year at Illinois University. He realised that architecture would not be as paying as the others. He believed that a dishwasher would earn more than he could earn in his home country.

Determined to become rich, he moved ahead to complete his graduation degree from the UIUC College of Engineering in 1971 in Industrial engineering. Khan started his first job at automotive manufacturing company Flex-N-Gate while attending the University of Illinois. As soon as he graduated, he joined as the engineering director for the company.

Shahid Khan soon blueprinted a company named Bumper Works. The company made one-piece truck bumper that cuts down weight along with adding structural support. Bumper Works went ahead to acquire Flex-N-Gate in 1980 from his former employer Charles Gleason Butzow. The company has a substantial share and brand name in the automobile sector. After the success of the venture, Khan gained a US citizenship in 1991.

His real time net worth is $4.5 million dollars.

In 2011, Khan invested money in National Football league team. He invested in Jacksonville Jaguars from Wayne Weaver. Moving ahead in the year 2013, he invested his fortune buying the London soccer club Fulham of the Premier League.

A passionate sportsman by nature and true American at heart make him one of the most influential personalities in the country.

He is an example of what determination could do in conjuction with focus and hard work, so my dear readers it's how you spend your 8760 that determine what you'll become. Will you choose to spend it on improving your world or complaining about the world around you

Kirk Kerkorian

Kirk kerkorian dropped out of school in the eighth grade to become a boxer.

Net worth: $3.9 billion (as of Sept. 2013)

Kirk Kerkorian was born in Fresno, California in 1917, on June 6th. Having Faced quite a variety phases of life, he stood against the odds and wrote his own classic, rags-to-riches success story. He dropped out from school after 8th grade and started practicing boxing to participate in the Pacific amateur welterweight championship. In 1939, he met Ted O'Flaherty who once invited him to sit by him and fly a plane. Though reluctant, Kirk agreed and the experience was so amazing that he ended up getting a commercial pilot license from Happy Bottom Riding Club. His flying expenses were born by Pancho Barnes, a renowned aviatrix, who, in return, asked him to take care of his farm and cattle.

After the World War II, he spent his savings $5000 on a Cessna, an aircraft manufacturer. He started working as a general aviation pilot and went to Las Vegas where he spent some time. In 1947, he paid $60,000 for a small air-charter service, Trans International Airlines, which would provide service to gamblers to fly Los Angeles to Las Vegas. In 1968, he sold it to the Transamerica Corporation for $104 million. And he moved to another business of purchasing and selling movie studios MGM Mirage which he sold to United Artist, Ted Turner. But extreme financial pressure forced Ted Turner to sell it back to Kirk Kerkorian. In 1990, the company was again owned by Giancarlo Parretti, an Italian financer and within six years in 1996, it came back to him. Finally he sold it to Sony in 2005 for $5 billion.

Kirk prefers to live a private life and for most of the time keeps himself away from public appearance. He has donated over $200 million through his charitable foundation. Through Lincy Foundation, he has donated $180 million to Armenia for which he was titled the Medal of Fatherland, the title carries the honor of national hero.

According to Forbes magazine of 2008, he was the 41th richest business man whose net worth is $16 billion. But, disastrous recession did not spare him and his rank in billionaire list dropped tremendously. Recently is the 307th richest across the world, remember we have 8760 hours in a year, how do you choose to spend yours.

John Paul DeJoria

the man behind a hair-care empire and Patron Tequila, once lived in a foster home and his car.

Net worth: $4 billion (as of Sept. 2013)

In Washington D.C., John Paul DeJoria was inducted into the prestigious Horatio Alger Association of Distinguished Americans, joining the ranks of other uber-successfuls such as former Secretaries of State, Colin Powell and Henry Kissinger, Oprah Winfrey, Norman Vincent Peale, J.C. Penny, and billionaire entrepreneur, Wayne Huizenga. It was a momentous occasion for a man who was homeless - twice.

A well-known jetsetter, environmentalist, philanthropist, and multi-millionaire entrepreneur, John Paul DeJoria is frequently seen with friends Kevin Costner, Cher, Michael Douglas, Pierce Brosnan, Fran Dresher, Robert Kennedy, Jr., Sir Richard Branson, and just about every other famous name we could mention, traveling via private jet to any of his six homes scattered around the U.S. — one as big as a shopping mall. While chatting with J.P., as close friends call him, relaxing at his home in Austin, Texas, we uncovered some interesting insights into his secrets of success.

Early childhood was pretty rough for DeJoria, the youngest son of immigrant parents who relocated from Italy and Greece, hoping to find the American Dream. "My parents were divorced before I was two years old. My brother and I started selling Christmas cards and newspapers when I was nine years old. I'd get up at three in the morning with my brother, to fold and deliver papers every morning just so we could live a little better," recalls J.P. His goals were simpler then, "When I was a kid, my dream was to be able to get a job where one day I could make $150 a week – enough for a small house payment, and a good used car."

Not unlike other youth growing up in the lower income barios of East Los Angeles, DeJoria soon found himself part of a street gang. But upon graduation from high school, he chose a different path, and enlisted in the U.S. Navy with aspirations of attending college. After his discharge, a brief marriage left young J.P. alone to raise his son as a single parent. Times went from bad to worse. "It was one of the most frightening times in my life," says DeJoria. "I was homeless twice, mainly because I was too proud to ask anybody for help. In my early twenties, when it was just me and my son, we had no place to live. I used to go out and collect Coke bottles at night, then cash them in at the corner drugstore for two to five cents. We lived on a very simple diet of rice, potatoes, lettuce, cereal, canned soup, and macaroni and cheese, but we managed."

He took on a variety of odd jobs to make ends meet from pumping gas and repairing bicycles, to selling encyclopedias door-to-door, then copy machines, and even insurance. As luck would have it, he was offered an entry-level marketing position with Time magazine. Before long, he found himself the Los Angeles circulation manager, well on the way to his next brush with fate. By 1971, he went to work for Redken Laboratories, then the leading professional hair salon product company in the U.S. Within 18 months, he was promoted to national manager overseeing their schools and chain salons, eagerly learning everything there was to know about the business.

Then in 1980, DeJoria jumped at the chance to join forces with longtime friend, and famed hair designer, Paul Mitchell, who had carved out a niche for himself by catering to New York's upper echelon of rock-and-rollers, models, writers, artists and celebrities before moving to the opposite end of the spectrum — and landing in Hawaii. Neither had much in the way of material wealth at the time, but they managed to scrape together $700 to initially bankroll the company with Paul doing the hair shows, and J.P. overseeing all the sales, marketing, administration, and everything else. The rest is, as they say, history.

Today, DeJoria heads the multi-million dollar hair empire of John Paul Mitchell Systems with annual retail sales well over $800 million, offering more than 90 products sold in 105,000 hair salons throughout the U.S. and in 75 countries abroad. When not working to expand the JPM brand, JP travels the globe with wife, Eloise and son, John Anthony as stuards of the planet.

 So, what is the secret to this tremendous success? DeJoria's golden rule of "Success unshared is failure," runs true throughout the company. Sources from within say that it is a place where people joyfully show up for work as opposed to merely showing up to collect a paycheck. And, he has gone to great lengths to create an atmosphere of success by hiring only the very best people, asking for them to give 110%, and then compensating them higher than what the industry normally pays to let them know their work is valued. His management philosophy is to have "fewer moving parts with no middle management." Effectively, JPMS does with 160 employees (worldwide) what would normally be done by six or seven hundred employees in any other firm.

Always a trend setter in corporate negotiations, DeJoria admits that "leisure hours are my working way of life. For example, I'll have lunch with a distributor, and I will bring my wife and son along. They really like family values. Then, before you know it, they are asking for me to bring Eloise and John Anthony along." J.P. has his own ideas on how to deal with difficult people too, "Sometimes, the best thing to do is to have nothing to do with them at all, unless you have to, because you really have to like the people you are dealing with. You know how, sometimes, you feel weird around someone? Follow your instincts – split and run the other way!"

DeJoria considers himself lucky to be surrounded with so many high-powered, fun-loving friends in life. "The difference between successful people, and unsuccessful people, is that the successful people are willing to do the things that unsuccessful people won't do," he confidently states. Now that he has reached a pinnacle of success, and is frequently asked to donate to everyone, and everything, he remains discriminating, "You can't help everyone out. So, you have to pick and choose what you want to do because you can't do it all!"

Yet, when asked what ranked so high on his list that without it, life wouldn't be worth it, he ⬜uickly replied, "Happiness….because if you're not happy with what you're doing, life just isn't worth living."

This is a great lesson to us that I conjuction with determination, you need to do what makes you happy, I mean what you are happy doing, don't settle for GOOD go for the BEST. Back to 8760 hours isbwhat we have in a year, how do you choose to spend yours. Will you choose to spend it on improving your world or complaining about the world around you

Do Won Chang

Do Won Chang worked as a janitor, gas station attendant, and in a coffee shop when he first moved to America.

Net worth: $5 billion (as of Sept. 2013)

Growing up in South Korea, Do Won Chang had to work three jobs as a janitor, gas station employee, and coffee shop attendant to support his family when they moved from Korea to America in 1981 at age 18, he figured hot joe would be his ticket to the American dream. Flashy Mercedes-Benzes and BMWs changed his mind. "I noticed the people who drove the nicest cars were all in the garment business," Chang said.

After three years of thrift-spending, he was able to open his first retail store Fashion 21, which grew to be the retail clothing giant Forever 21, a pioneer in fast fashion.

The economic downturn forced Chang to make some cuts. The company ended 2009 with seven fewer stores than the year before. Still, revenue is climbing. In the last fiscal year, Forever 21 posted $1.7 billion in sales. It projects revenue of $2.3 billion this year. Much of that is from aggressive expansion — Chang is eyeing Israel and Hong Kong, for example. E ually important is a broad lineup. In addition to Forever 21, the chain has seven other formats, each serving distinct breeds of mall rats, including XXI Forever, which focuses on higher end couture lines, and Heritage 1981, featuring vintage-styled clothes.

The multinational clothing empire with over 480 outlets worldwide generates an annual income of $3 billion.

START SMALL: Most great businesses started small, start your big dream small.

The question is do you have a clear cut vision of how you want to spend your 8760 hours in a year and are you willing to pay the price? Which is determination, focus and hard work through which you can be successful regardles of your background,believe, race and education.

NOTE: This idea of just winning a "Big Contract" or Getting "Stupendous Wealth" overnight that wasn't worked hard for isn't going to happen...

So start thinking and start moving.

Ralph Lauren

Ralph lauren was once a clerk at Brooks Brothers dreaming of men's ties.

Net worth: $7.7 billion (as of Sept. 2013)

With a net worth of $6.5 billion, it's hard to imagine that Ralph Lauren's luxury label and privileged lifestyle is a far cry away from his modest upbringing.

But in the recent documentary, Bloomberg's Game Changers: Ralph Lauren, the richest man in American fashion reveals the struggles of his youth growing up as part of a Jewish immigrant working-class family.

Youngest of four children, Ralph Lauren or Ralph Lifshitz, shared a bedroom with his brothers, whilst growing up in the Bronx, New York in the 1940s and 50s.

At the age of 12, he worked after school to fund his extravagant taste in clothing and was known for selling hand-made ties to his fellow students at school - little did he know this would become the driving force of his entrepreneurial success.

He would spend his afternoons as a teenager at the cinema dreaming of a better life. And this dream of fantasy and fiction translated into the designer's later work which was influenced by actors such as Fred Astaire and Cary Grant.

Michael Gross, author of the biography Genuine Authentic: The Real Life of Ralph Lauren says "that vision, that ability to step into a fantasy world, Ralph bought to the fashion business."

Ralph's love for elegant style and fine living was rivalled only by his drive for success. And this determination to step away from his childhood misfortune was ever present from an early age.

The Daily Telegraph published an article in 1986 that "he doesn't like talking about his roots, but his towering ambition discovered itself early: Asked to list his goals in the De Witt Clinton High school's class of 1957 yearbook, Ralph wrote: 'millionaire."

But after leaving the army in 1964, the designer worked as a sales clerk at Brooks Brothers. He married receptionist Ricky

Low-Beer, who is still his wife, and moved to New York to live his American dream.

It was only by 1967 that he started designing and making professional ties after having gained fashion experience at Rivetz & Co. His innovative wide tie designs made over half a million dollars.

And following the release of his infamous Ralph Lauren polo shirt in 1972, the designer was transformed from cinema dreamer to worldwide fashion mogul.

It had taken him two decades to progress from his first low-payed job as a glove salesman to multi-millionaire status.

Since then Ralph Lauren's brand has rocketed with over 300 stores in the US and 100 others worldwide. All collections boast the label's renowned all American-style which combines easy-to-wear pieces in luxurious materials and fashion-forward ensembles.

Ralph once asked: "People ask how can a Jewish kid from the Bronx do preppy clothes? Does it have to do with class and money? It has to do with dreams." And influenced by this sense of dream, the 79-year-old's impressive empire has earned his style icon status.

His motto 'we don't sell an item, we sell a way of life' certainly proved a point. The living legend stands for a dream - and it was a dream that certainly came true.

As the 122nd wealthiest man in the world, the fashion designer resides a deluxe home on Fifth Avenue, New York. He also owns beach resorts in Jamaica and Montauk, Long Island and despite his advancing years is still a regular on the US social scene.

mogul Francois Pinault

Mogul Francois Pinault quit high school in 1974 after being bullied for being poor.

Net worth: $15 billion (as of March 2013)

Believing in what negative people think of you or giving in to self-limiting thoughts is the biggest obstruction to success. People who channelize negative comments into changing their lives are winners; French business mogul and art collector Francois Pinault is one of them.

Things went worst for Francois Pinault when he was consistently teased for being poor in high school by his fellow students and he finally opted to drop out. He turned the negative experiences of his life into a stream of positive energies, altered those negative words made against him into positive ones and proceeded in life with determination, consistency, and hard work. Difficult life situations made him learn to deal with them head on and he ended up becoming the man behind some the world's famous high-fashion houses including Stella McCartney, Alexander McQueen, and YSL.

After quitting his high school in 1947, he joined his family's business – timber trading. In the 1970s when he already had the knowledge of how to keep going on with business he started buying smaller firms and transforming them into giant enterprise. His strategy in taking over small enterprises and turning them into mega brands has helped him to establish the sprawling empire. Today his net worth stands over $15 billion.

His story is inspiring for those who believe in dreaming big and keeping faith that they do come true with perseverance and sincere hard work. Critics or doubters can't take your courage away if you stay strong enough to stand firm, regardless of circumstances, regardless of your status, background or tribe, it's how you spend your 8760 hours in a year that counts. Will you choose to spend it on improving your world or complaining about the world around you.

Leonardo Del Vecchio

Leonardo Del Vecchio grew up in an orphanage and later worked in a factory where he lost part of his finger.

Net worth: $15.3 billion (as of March 2013)

True is the saying. It is just the dictionary that tolerates success to come before rigorous hard work and effort. Success comes to those who work towards it without caring about the conse uences, the obstacles, the efforts and the time it takes. They cannot see any of these issues in their path. All they see is their goal shinning, high, like a prized trophy and they just want to grab it.

Aren't we all eager to buy the latest launch of these cool, always trending, sunglasses? They are so-in-trend, stylish, funky, and an important part of projecting a certain lifestyle. But have we ever even imagined how they became the brand that they are?

Leonardo-Del-Vecchio was one of five orphans whose widowed mother was helpless due to poverty and had to abandon her children. Beginning his life, and growing up in an orphanage, never was easy for Vecchio. Imagine as a kid, how much he would have suffered and felt as if the world was stacked against him. How many Christmases were there with no family gatherings but just the regular orphanage routine, whatever that may be?

He grew up and got a job at a factory that made the molded parts for automobiles and eyeglass frames. Sadly enough, while working in the factory he lost a part of his finger too but none of these incidents stopped him. He kept working hard.

At 23 years of age he was successful enough to open his own eyeglass shop which today has turned into one of the largest company of eyeglasses or prescription based eye-wear. Once a grief-stricken orphanage child, today he owes a grand empire of over 6000 stores worldwide that are worth over $11.5 billion.

Now that's what I call success. People like this are hard to not admire, as they truly deserve it. Not only are these the bigger examples, but also the smaller examples exist all around us. Kids from tough environments find ways to earn prestigious university scholarships, orphans who are ill-fated or abused. These are also real successes. The only thing that matters is strong determination. You dictate what you will become, not your initial circumstance.

You muse accept everything that stands in the way of success as a challenge and another opportunity to prove yourself. You must not allow any of it to become a demotivating factor that you can use as an excuse to blame for failure. The choice to succeed is yours.

Success comes to those who believe they can.

Li Ka-shing

Li Ka-Shing had to ⬜uit school to help support his family after the death of his father.

Net worth: $31 billion (as of March 2013)

When Li Ka-Shing was just 14 years old, his father died of tuberculosis. In order to earn money for his family, Li was forced to abandon school and take a job at a plastics factory. The family was so poor that Le actually had to sell his dead father's clothes for cash to pay for food. While most of his piers attended school or played games, Li labored away for 16 hours a day making plastic watchbands. Sounds terrible, right? Well if it makes you feel any better, today Li Ka-Shing is the richest person in Asia with a personal net worth of $30 billion. In fact, thanks to some extremely shrewd investments, he has been a billionaire for over a ⬜uarter of a century! Li Ka-Shing's rise to obscene levels of wealth and power is a truly inspirational rags to riches story.

Li Ka-Shing was born on June 13, 1928 in Chaozhou, Guangdong, China. While Li was in elementary school, it was a common occurrence for the Japanese to drop bombs on Chaozhu, so his family took refuge in Hong Kong. Li's father was a school principal, but tragically succumbed to tuberculosis shortly after the family arrived and settled in their new adopted home country.

Li was also infected with tuberculosis. The isolation during this recovery, coupled with such extreme poverty and feelings of helplessness, had a deep impact on Li Ka-Shing. Dealing with a war, the loss of a parent, severe illness, and poverty all before the age of 15, instilled a lifelong drive to succeed beyond into the future tycoon.

As we mentioned earlier, Li was forced to quit school at the age of 15 to work as an apprentice in a factory that made plastic watch straps. By the time we was 14, he had a full time job in a plastics trading company and was a big help in supporting his family. In 1950, at the age of 22, Li quit his job to start his own company that made plastic toys. The company soon changed shifted plans and instead began producing plastic flowers because he heard how popular they were in Italy. It was Li's first savvy business decision. He named this company Cheung Kong. Fast forward to the present and Cheung Kong is one of the largest real estate investment companies in the world.

Around this same time, Li began buying apartment buildings and factories throughout Hong Kong with every extra penny he manged to save. Because this was a period of severe social unrest marked by Maoist-led riots and bombings, Li often able to purchase real estate at steep discounts. By the time the market recovered from the social instability, Li started to make a killing. In 1979 he became the first Chinese citizen to acquire a controlling stake in an old British trading house, Hutchison Whampoa. Because Hutchison Whampoa had been struggling for years, Li shrewdly convinced Hongkong & Shanghai Bank (HSBC) to sell him their 22% stake in the company for less than half the book value. Hutchison Whampoa owned shipyards, docks, vast parcels of retail space and much more, mainly throughout Hong Kong. Over the next decade, Li managed to successfully turn Hutchison Whampoa around and expand its empire throughout the world. Today, Hutchison Whampoa is one of the most valuable companies in the world with annual revenues of over $50 billion.

Li's office at the top of Cheung Kong Center in central Hong Kong has a private pool and one of the fastest elevators in the world. You can ascend 70 stories in less than 45 seconds.

By 1987, Li had transformed himself from factory worker to full fledged billionaire. That same year, Li and his partners paid $500 million to acquire roughly half of Husky Oil, a Canadian company that consistently lost money and had been through many restructurings and mergers. The timing of this acquisition could not have been any more perfect. At the time of the purchase, a barrel of oil traded for roughly $10. Over the next thirty years, a single barrel rose from $10, to $30, to $50 to an all time high of $140. Today, a single barrel of oil sells for $93 which helps Husky Energy generate over $25 billion a year in revenue. Li still has a stake in the company which is worth over $8 billion on its own.

Throughout his life, Li continued to invest in real estate and a diverse range of other industries. Li's companies handle 70% of Hong Kong's port traffic, have huge stakes in the electric companies and mobile phone services—in a way, you could say he controls Hong Kong from the top of his tower. But beyond real estate, Li Ka-Shing has shown an uncanny perception for the tech-world. The octogenarian took about five minutes in late 2007 to decide to invest $120 million in Facebook. Keep in mind that back in 2007, Facebook barely made any money. It had only recently opened up to membership beyond college students, and Myspace had just proven to be a disastrous investment for Rupert Murdoch's Newscorp. Today, that 0.8% stake in Facebook is worth $900 million.

Li also invested in Skype in 2005 when it was losing money. A year later, eBay paid $2.5 billion for it. Li also backed Siri, which, as we all know was bought by Apple in 2010. Li is also invested millions of dollars into Spotify, Waze and HzO. Oh and by the way, after he invested in Spotify, he reportedly told the company Spotify needed to be in his car. This was 2009, long before Spotify had a mobile app. Li's technology investments display a particular brilliance with understand not just where the tech world is, but where it is going. He believes in technology that is a game changer. Things like Facebook, Waze, Siri, etc. His investments have been so savvy, that people began referring to Li-Ka Shing as "Superman". He is even frequently depicted as so in newspapers and magazines.

But Li still invests in more traditional business as well. In fact in 2010, Li Ka-Shing's Cheung Kong made its biggest acquisition to date when it bought U.K. Power Networks for $9.1 billion. This means that Li now supplies about eight million Brits with power. In 2011, Li bought Northumbrian Water, which ferries clean drinking water to 4.5 million people in England and provides sewerage services to another 2.7 million.

Basically, wherever you look, Li Ka-Shing is there in some way. Or so it seems. When Li's tech investments don't pan out, he personally takes the financial hit. When the tech investments hit a windfall, he puts the profits into his Li Ka-Shing Foundation, which he refers to as his third son. The foundation has donated more than $1.6 billion, mostly to education. He has given $690 million to create Shantou University. He donated $40 million to Berkeley for a new biomedical research facility.

Today, thanks largely to his majority stakes in Cheung Kong, Hutchison Whampoa and various other investment, Li-Ka Shing is worth $30 billion. That's far and away enough to make him the richest person in Asia and the 18th richest person in the world! Not bad for a former dirt poor factory worker!

Harold Simmons

Harold Simmons grew up in a shack with no plumbing or electricity.

Net worth: $40 billion (as of Sept. 2013)

He's been called Dallas' Most Evil Genius by amassing a fortune even without anyone knowing. He is known to live his life in obscurity but even at age 78, he wouldn't stop thinking of how he'd earn his next billion dollar fortune. He's an entrepreneur, a success story for a generation to follow. He's authoritative and bold, even to the point of calling President Obama a dangerous man. But that's the kind of man he was – soft spoken for a man of his talent and rich but not affluent in lifestyle.

We could all learn from his life story. His name was Harold Clark Simmons - a businessman and investor in Dallas, Texas. For someone whose net worth was $10 Billion by the time he died in 2013, he lived a rather reclusive life. He rarely grants interviews by media especially when he was beginning to age. But that didn't mean he stopped working a day in his life. He just did it quietly, without need of flashing his own success story. History did all the talking for him.

How Simmons Grew Up

The story of Harold Simmons is known around the Dallas rich and famous circuit. That's because of his humble beginnings as an entrepreneur. He may have amassed a wealth of billions but his birth was far from the life of affluence people knew he lived. He grew up in a small rural town of Golden, Texas where his home had no electricity or running water.

He wasn't born rich and so he didn't grow up thinking he could be. His family was focused on surviving the harsh life of labor. In all of his life, what was most important was hard work. But he was driven by it. He knew it might pay off in the end. He earned his educational merits because his parents were teachers and eventually graduated from the University of Texas in Austin with a master's degree in economics.

He then went on to work as a bank examiner for the U.S. government before his talents and genius in banking was acquired by a Dallas-based Republic National Bank. Later in his life, he would use his expertise to develop a business acquisition technique called leveraged buyout where he earned a fortune on its practice.

How He Became a Millionaire

In 1961, he put his money where his brain was. He thought that he could make something high-rolling out of a small investment. So he used up a $5,000 of lifesavings and a loan of $95,000 to buy a drugstore. It was not real estate, but a drugstore chain with a very promising future. After 12 years and 100 stores into his name, he sold his initial investment and turned it into a $50 million payout.

This payday was the start of a lucrative career in investment. Later on, he acquired more companies including Amalgamated Sugar, Lockheed Corporation, McDermott International and Muse Air by acquiring and selling investment. He believed he was a corporate "builder" because his record is one that develops a company before he sells them.

Today, he is survived by companies called Contran Corporation and Valhi, Inc. which has a combined worth of $7 Billion in assets. Simmons has also controlled 5 companies traded in the New York Stock Exchange. He's a Texan by heart and although he was mostly a recluse, he donated several of his fortunes to charities, schools and other worthy non-profits in Dallas. The billionaire reportedly donated $175 Million to the Simmons Cancer Center in Dallas Texas. You'll see his memorial at the Winspear Opera House where a facade of windows under the name Annette and Harold Simmons would remind you of the kind of man he was.

Lessons from the life of Harold Simmons

- Never be afraid to voice out your opinions
- Hard work pays off in the end
- There is no need to boast about your achievements and wealth
- Keeping a low profile is sometimes good
- Master a niche and make a fortune by specializing

Oracle's Larry Ellison

Larry Ellison dropped out of college after his adoptive mother died and held odd jobs for eight years.

Net worth: $41 billion (as of Sept. 2013)

You may not have heard about Larry Ellison but you may certainly have heard about Oracle. This multi-billion software company was started by this billionaire. Ellison is currently the 5th richest person in the world with a net worth of $49 Billion. You may not know this, but the movie Iron Man was based on the life of this man. The next time you watch the Iron Man movies again, try and spot Oracle signs and building. You may also spot him doing a cameo appearance in Iron Man 2.

Born in the Bronx, Larry Ellison had a difficult childhood. His mother was only 19 years old and single, so she gave Larry to his uncle and aunt to raise. Moved to Chicago, Ellison grew up in a small two-bedroom apartment. He found out that he was adopted when he was 12 years old. Around this time, his adoptive father lost his business due to the Depression and started working as an auditor. Rebellious and independent-minded, Larry Ellison showed an aptitude for science.

After dropping out of the University of Illinois, he transferred to the University of Chicago before dropping out a semester later. This constant changing of schools caused his adoptive father to believe that Larry would never learn anything with his life. Instead, Ellison began to learn about computer programming. After saving up enough money for gas, Ellison decided to move to Berkeley, California. He switched jobs frequently for eight years before working on a mainframe system with Amdahl Corporation.

By 1977, Ellison decided to create a company with his co-workers, Ed Oates and Robert Miner. They named their new business, Software Development Labs. After reading a paper about a Structured Query Language, Larry started working on a range of new projects.

His company was hired by the CIA to build Oracle. They completed the project one year early and used the remaining time to figure out commercial applications. This relational database management system (RDBMS) was named Oracle as well. By 1981, IBM chose to adopt Oracle and Oracle's sales doubled. For the next seven years, sales doubled annually. This success with Oracle led to Ellison renaming the business Oracle Company.

In 1986, Oracle finally went public. The initial public offering served to raise $31.5 million. By 1990, the company reported its first losses due to years of overstated revenue. This caused the market capitalization to drop by 80 percent and pushed Oracle to the edge of bankruptcy. To keep the company solvent, Ellison fired top level employees and brought in more experienced managers. Larry Ellison used this change as an opportunity to step back from management and focus more on product development. Oracle 7 was released in 1992 and the company's fortunes started to improve.

Throughout the 1990s, a range of financial institutions, retail businesses and automobile companies turned to Oracle for database programs. Due to this, Ellison was encouraged to find business applications for Oracle online. As ecommerce sites grew, net profits increased. In one ⬜uarter in 2000, the profits jumped by 76 percent. This caused Larry Ellison to surpass Bill Gates as the world's richest man at that time.

Starting in 2004, Ellison worked to increase Oracle's market share by acquiring a range of other companies. After purchasing Sun Microsystems in 2009, Oracle became the biggest software company in the world. Larry Ellison has served as the president of Oracle from 1978 to 1996 and brief time periods as the

Chairman of the Board. Since the early beginnings of Oracle, Ellison has been the company's only CEO.

Lessons from the life of Larry Ellison

- He was adopted and his real parents was not with him in his childhood. Yet he was able to rise above this difficulty and became successful.
- When your business is facing bankruptcy and difficulties, be willing to keep within your budget.
- Find good and talented employees and talents to help your struggling business.
- To grow fast, a business should acquire companies that will benefit them.

Andrew Carnegie

Long after he had established himself as one of America's leading businessmen, as well as history's greatest steelmaker, Andrew Carnegie reflected that "We all live in the richest and freest country in the world, where no man is limited except by his own mental attitude and his own desires."

At the time—a decade or so before the First World War—Carnegie's attitude was nearly universal. In America, anyone could carve out a better life for himself if he worked hard. Today, Carnegie's attitude is considered almost quaint.

It's hard to imagine anyone beginning in a lower station. Carnegie had arrived in America, a twelve-year-old Scottish immigrant. With barely a penny to his family's name, and with only five years of formal education behind him ("Lack of schooling is no valid excuse for failure; neither is an exhaustive schooling a guarantee of success," he would later say), young Andrew went to work at a textile mill, twelve hours a day, for $1.20 a week.

It wasn't much, but it was enough. The job gave Carnegie the opportunity to learn and to demonstrate his dedication to hard work. Very quickly he moved on and up: less than a year later he had secured a position at O'Reilly's Telegraph Company, starting at more than twice what he had earned at the mill.

It was there that Carnegie's rise began in earnest—not through some "lucky break" but through the habit Carnegie would later refer to as "going the extra mile." Carnegie, still working incredibly long days, began going to work early in order to learn how to send and receive telegraph messages. He worked so hard at it that he could eventually take telegraph messages by ear rather than by transcribing the Morse code—a feat only two other people in America could perform.

That ability helped him gain the notice of Thomas A. Scott, a superintendent for the Pennsylvania Railroad. Scott hired the young man, still a teenager, to be his secretary and telegrapher at $35 a month—a tidy sum at the time and a far cry from $1.20 a week.

Carnegie soon became indispensable to Scott. The real turning point came not too long after he was hired. Carnegie was in the office alone one day when news came of a wreck on the Eastern Division. Rail traffic started backing up; instead of shrugging his shoulders and saying "not my job, not my problem," Carnegie chose to take action. "Mr. Scott was not to be found," he would later write. "Finally, I could not resist the temptation to plunge in, take the responsibility, give 'train orders' and set matters going."

It was no easy decision. Although Carnegie had watched Scott deal with similar problems in the past, lives and property were at stake. "I knew it was dismissal, disgrace, perhaps criminal punishment for me if I erred. On the other hand, I could bring in the wearied freight-train men who had lain out all night. I could set everything in motion. I knew I could." And he did, forging Scott's signature and issuing orders until rail traffic was back to normal.

Thanks to Carnegie's determination and hard-won abilities, Scott started opening doors for the young man and teaching him the skills he would need to succeed in business. Later, he would help Carnegie make his first investment, launching Andrew's career as a capitalist in earnest. By 1860, at the age of 25, Carnegie was making almost $50,000—more than enough to count himself as wealthy.

"Opportunity" means a set of circumstances in which a course of successful action is possible. Opportunity is abundant. What's scarce is the willingness to take advantage of it. To the extent a country is free, a person with no money, no education, no connections can rise as far as his ability and ambition will take him. But developing ability and ambition is a challenging, uncomfortable, even scary process. Relatively few people in any era choose to do it, and as a result, few capitalize on life's unlimited opportunities.

In Carnegie's words, a "man may be born in poverty, but he does not have to go through life in poverty. He may be illiterate but he does not have to remain so. But . . . no amount of opportunity will benefit the man who neglects or refuses to take possession of his own mind power and use it for his own personal advancement."

That was what led Carnegie to success: the constant use of his mind in pursuit of a better life. Whether he was learning a new skill, taking decisive action in an emergency, or forging the most innovative and efficient steelmaking company in the world, the commitment to following the judgment of his reasoning mind was the only opportunity he needed.

That—the willingness to think—is something no one else can give you.

Want to suceed in life it's how you spend your 8760 hours in a year that count, Will you choose to spend it on improving your world or complaining about the world around you

Quotes from succesfull people

"If you are not willing to risk the usual, you will have to settle for the ordinary." - *Jim Rohn*

Take up one idea. Make that one idea your life -- think of it, dream of it, live on that idea. Let the brain, muscles, nerves, every part of your body be full of that idea, and just leave every other idea alone. This is the way to success." -- *Swami Vivekananda*

All our dreams can come true if we have the courage to pursue them." - *Walt Disney*

"Success is walking from failure to failure with no loss of enthusiasm." - **Winston Churchill**

"Someone is sitting in the shade today because someone planted a tree a long time ago." -- **Warren Buffett**

"You only live once, but if you do it right, once is enough." -- **Mae West**

"Opportunities don't happen. You create them." -- **Chris Grosser**

"There is no easy walk to freedom anywhere, and many of us will have to pass through the valley of the shadow of death again and again before we reach the mountaintop of our desires." -- **Nelson Mandela**

"The difference between winning and losing is most often not quitting." - **Walt Disney**

I have not failed. I've just found 10,000 ways that won't work." -- **Thomas Edison**

"Failure is another steppingstone to greatness." -- **Oprah Winfrey**

"If you're going through hell, keep going." -- **Winston Churchill**

"To me, business isn't about wearing suits or pleasing stockholders. It's about being true to yourself, your ideas and focusing on the essentials."--**Richard Branson**

"Start where you are. Use what you have. Do what you can." -- **Arthur Ashe**

"Don't limit yourself. Many people limit themselves to what they think they can do. You can go as far as your mind lets you. What you believe, remember, you can achieve."-**Mary Kay Ash**

"Success is the sum of small efforts, repeated day-in and day-out." - **Robert Collier**

To most people, being born in a free country is the greatest gift. To others, it's a fleeting thought. For the latter, I feel sorry.

Before I go any further, I must admit that not everyone will find success. There will always be those who sit around waiting for success to find them. There will be those who are simply not willing to achieve it. And then there's the fact that success would not exist without failure. All of these things create what we know; a world where success and failure are experienced by different groups of people.

Everyone in a free country has the opportunity to succeed. So why doesn't everyone succeed? Because success and failure are choices made consciously and subconsciously and failure is chosen by many for various reasons.

Here are 7 undeniable reasons why some people fail where others succeed

1. They Define Success Wrong

"Striving for success without hard work is like trying to harvest where you haven't planted." – *David Bly*

Do you believe that success is won, innate, or earned? The answer someone gives can tell you a lot about them, and why they are where they are.

Success is won: if you believe that success is won, you experience animosity and envy toward those you view as lucky or more fortunate than you. You also believe that success is out of your control; it simply depends on a flip of the coin or certain circumstances.

How hard are you willing to work if you believe that success is won rather than earned?

Success is innate: people who believe success is innate often feel the same as those who believe it's won. The only difference is that believers in innate-success have a more pessimistic view of opportunity; it's trivial to them (we'll go over this a little later). Why does opportunity matter if success is innate?

How hard are you willing to work if you feel your opportunity doesn't matter and your chances of success are nil because of your circumstances?

Success is earned: the last group of people believes what we know to be true based on statistical analysis; success is earned. These people understand that in order to succeed, they must earn it. How do they earn it? They climb the mountain and utilize the same process others have used to achieve.

How hard are you willing to work if you believe success must be earned? Your 8760 hours will tell.

2. They Define Opportunity Wrong

"The ladder of success is best climbed by stepping on the rungs of opportunity." – **Ayn Rand**

Do you believe that opportunity provides a possibility of success, a probability of success, or that it's trivial?

Let's ask the same questions we asked when we discussed success:

How hard are you willing to work if you believe the opportunity you were born with is trivial?

How hard are you willing to work if you believe the opportunity you were born with is a possibility?

How hard are you willing to work if you believe the opportunity you were born with is a probability?

I hope this is coming together for you. I still want to go further though. I want you to see exactly how your views on opportunity and success work together to help determine your outcome.

People who believe success is won see their opportunity as a possibility, but sometimes as trivial.

People who believe success is innate see their opportunity as trivial.

People who believe success is earned see their opportunity as a probability, but sometimes only as a possibility.

In layman's terms, the rich see success as earned and view their opportunity as probability. The middle class see success as earned and view their opportunity as possibility, but sometimes as probability. The poor class sees success as won or innate and views their opportunity as trivial, or in some cases as a possibility, but not a probability.

Of course, people don't stay in one class their entire life. The people who move between classes tend to have the same outlook as those of the class they move to.

3. They Define Work Wrong

"The value of a man's position is often determined by the number of people qualified to fill it." – **Kevin Geary**

We just discussed two important terms: success and opportunity. In order to continue our discussion further, we must discuss another, "work."

"But success doesn't always come from hard work!"

Inevitably, people will point out that factory employees work harder than CEOs. Of course, this depends on your analysis of the word "work."

Choose a corresponding term:

- Physical Labor
- Mental Labor

Those who claim that success doesn't always come from hard work only acknowledge one aspect of work, physical labor.

Of course, work is labor, period. Excluding mental labor from the term work is biased and unfair. CEOs may sit at a desk, wear a suit, and enjoy the air conditioning, but that doesn't mean they labor any less than the man in the shop room, it's simply a different type of labor. Not accepting this is like making the argument that one who hates their job labors more than one who enjoys their job and the pay should be altered to make up for it. You see where this is going?

In terms of pay scale, people who run companies are worth a lot more than those who assemble products. Why? Because it's easy to find people who can assemble products and it's not very easy to find people who can operate multi-million dollar companies for a profit.

Needless to say, the man in the shop room wouldn't have a job if the CEO behind the desk wasn't doing his (and vice versa). The only difference is which job you'd rather be doing, and that depends solely on the choices you make throughout your life.

How do you think the CEO views success and opportunity? How do you think the shop worker views those same terms?

4. They Defeat Themselves

"To expect defeat is nine-tenths of defeat itself." – **Henry Mencken**

While there is a minority of people who actually choose to fail, the majority that fail simply make poor choices or have a poor outlook. Basically, for the majority, failure is a choice but not a decision.

I can't possibly list all of the bad choices people make which lead them to failure, but a few to get you headed in the right direction are:

- Abusing drugs or alcohol / addiction. .
- Having a poor work ethic.
- Having a child too young or out of wedlock.
- Immaturity / laziness.

- Borrowing too much money.

And the list goes on, and on, and on…..and on.

Of course, there are also those things which are out of someone's control.

If you're born into an inner-city family and attend a poor school system, you obviously start out behind others. If you're handicapped, your road to success may be longer and more difficult. But none of this bars you from success; I'll elaborate on this later when we discuss circumstances.

Lastly, as our quote up top reminds us, many people defeat themselves simply by expecting defeat in the first place. They don't expect success and it actually becomes a self-fulfilling prophecy. For more on this, you might like my highly popular article; Your Life Sucks Because You Expect it to Suck (and 10 Ways to Improve it Right Now).

5. They Think Failure is Final

"Success is the ability to go from failure to failure without losing your enthusiasm." – **Winston Churchill**

"But, hard work doesn't always equal success. Some people work really hard, but fail. They tried and didn't succeed."

Failure is a key ingredient in success. Those who don't achieve success most likely quit after their failure. Quitting, of course, is a choice.

If you were to follow in the footsteps of a successful person, you would likely pass the remnants of multiple failures. If you followed in the footsteps of a failure, you would find their lifeless future at the feet of their first opponent.

So the question is, how hard and for how long are you willing to fight? There are no shortcuts, statistically. The vast majority of millionaires are self-made and far too many lottery winners are broke and worse off than they were before they won the lottery. Why? Because wealth is about behavior and money doesn't protect you from failure.

If you want to succeed where other people fail, you have to step right over failure and keep walking. The people who don't make it let failure defeat them. Failure becomes their end result because they refuse to walk any further.

Look at it this way; if you aren't dead yet, there's still hope.

6. They're a Victim of Their Circumstances

"The first step toward success is taken when you refuse to be a captive of the environment in which you first find yourself." – *Mark Cain*

One of the biggest rebuttals given by non-achievers is that they are held back by their circumstances.

I don't think circumstance is a fair argument though. Yes, you may be subject to circumstances that make it more difficult for you to succeed, but that doesn't change the fact that you start with the same opportunity as others; the opportunity provided to you by living in a free country.

It's also important to note that some people handle circumstances better than others. For instance, you can't say that a handicap is a circumstance that prevents you from achieving when others with the same handicap have achieved.

Everyone has issues, circumstances, road blocks, etc. It's all about how you deal with your circumstances and how hard you're willing to work to overcome them. But the basics don't change; you're still in a free country and nobody is preventing you from achieving except for yourself.

Circumstance is also unimportant because it doesn't determine finality. For example, a trust fund baby can lose his fortune with a series of bad decisions just as easily as a child from the ghetto can acquire a fortune with a series of good decisions.

Don't be quick to judge others based on their circumstances. Instead, judge them based on their ferocity in overcoming those circumstances.

7. *They Take No For an Answer*

"Opposition is a natural part of life. Just as we develop our physical muscles through overcoming opposition – such as lifting weights – we develop our character muscles by overcoming challenges and adversity." – **Stephen R. Covey**

First, you are given an opportunity. Then, based on that opportunity, you hatch a dream. And when you try to execute that dream, you meet your opposition. It is here on the battleground, facing the opposition, that success is either realized or lost.

Everyone faces opposition on their way to the top. The crack babies and the trust fund babies both have their own sets of problems. And you can't assume that one faces more opposition than the other; everyone's life and path to success is unique.

The one thing they do have in common is the opportunity for success. But, as you try to succeed, there will be people and circumstances around every corner that try to tell you no. The disability you were born with tells you no, your abusive parents tell you no, your pessimistic friends tell you no, your lack of self esteem causes you to say no to yourself, addiction tells you no, and so on.

The people who succeed are those who don't take no for an answer. They shrug off the pessimism, they choose better friends, they put up boundaries with their family, and they surround themselves with positive people and things.

Conclusion

Success is possible for anyone who is willing to achieve it. There are many who want success, but there is a huge difference between wanting-to and willing-to. You have to be willing… I mean willing to spend your 8760 hours in a year the right way.

The other thing to remember is that your outlook and the way you define success, opportunity, and work play a large role in determining your outcome

Disclaimer

This book is not intended as a substitute for the medical advice of physicians. The reader should regularly consult a physician in matters relating to his/her health and particularly with respect to any symptoms that may require diagnosis or medical attention.

(health, maditation)

ABOUT THE AUTHOR

MY NAME IS -------------. i am

I really love educating people on how to stay healthy and live the life of their dreams.

Do not go yet; One last thing to do

If you enjoyed this book or found it useful I'd be very grateful if you'd post a short review on it. Your support really does make a difference and I read all the reviews personally so I can get your feedback and make this book even better.

Thanks again for your support!

www.ingramcontent.com/pod-product-compliance
Lightning Source LLC
Chambersburg PA
CBHW030505220526
45464CB00006B/2658